I.   Science, Technology, Engineering, and Mathematics (STEM) Education in the 2016 Budget

"America thrived in the 20th century because we made high school free, sent a generation of GIs to college, trained the best workforce in the world. We were ahead of the curve. But other countries caught on. And in a 21st century economy that rewards knowledge like never before, we need to up our game. We need to do more."

President Barack Obama
January 20, 2015

President Obama strongly believes that the United States must equip more students to excel in science, technology, engineering, and mathematics (STEM). That is why the President's 2016 Budget invests more than $3 billion, an increase of 3.8 percent over the 2015 enacted level, in STEM-education programs across the Federal Government. The 2016 Budget includes investments that will benefit students in a number of critical areas:

- Supporting more STEM-focused high schools, with a new $125 million competitive program at the Department of Education (ED) to help communities across America launch Next-Generation High Schools that will be laboratories for cutting-edge STEM teaching and learning.

- Preparing excellent STEM teachers, with $100 million in the 2016 Budget for high-quality teacher preparation within ED's new Teacher and Principal Pathways program, including a priority for STEM teacher preparation programs that make progress on the President's goal of preparing 100,000 excellent STEM teachers.

- Improving undergraduate STEM education, with the National Science Foundation (NSF) investing $135 million to improve: (1) retention of undergraduate STEM majors; and (2) undergraduate teaching and learning in STEM subjects to meet the President's goal of preparing 1 million more STEM graduates over a decade.

- Investing in breakthrough innovation research and development in education, with up to $50 million for the Advanced Research Projects Agency for Education (ARPA-ED), allowing ED to support rapid-cycle, high-impact research and development of next-generation learning technologies, including for STEM education.

In addition, with the overall number of STEM programs across the Federal Government already reduced by 40 percent over the past two years, the 2016 Budget continues efforts to reduce fragmentation among Federal STEM-education programs. It also focuses investment on the five key areas identified in the Federal STEM Education 5-Year Strategic Plan: K-12 instruction; undergraduate education; graduate education; broadening participation in STEM education and careers by women and minorities traditionally underrepresented in these fields; and STEM education activities that typically take place outside the classroom.

K-12 Education

The President's 2016 Budget includes investments to improve STEM education in K-12 schools, with a priority on supporting more inclusive STEM high schools and more rigorous STEM courses, training and supporting excellent STEM teachers, and scaling effective STEM programs.

Expanding Access to Rigorous STEM Courses

- Creating Next-Generation High Schools. The President has called for a whole-school transformation of the high school experience in order to provide students with challenging and relevant academic and career-related learning experiences that prepare them to transition to postsecondary education and careers. The 2016 Budget establishes a new $125 million competitive program at ED to help communities across America have the resources to launch Next-Generation High Schools that will be laboratories for cutting-edge STEM teaching and learning. These schools will showcase the tenets of high school reform that the President has championed – personalizing learning for students, strengthening relationships with business and post-secondary partners, and linking student work to real-world expectations and experiences that reflect college and careers – to better prepare students for their future. By placing a strong focus on projects designed to improve readiness for college and careers in STEM fields, the Administration will continue its efforts to address the equity gap in STEM education. Currently, a quarter of high schools with the highest percentage of African-American and Latino students do not even offer Algebra II, and a third fail to offer any chemistry. In addition, the Administration will convene a Summit on Next-Generation High Schools later in the year, and bring together the growing community of elected officials and leaders in education, business, and philanthropy committed to advancing high school reform. The Budget also supports a number of complementary investments in high school reform at ED: $556 million in School Improvement Grants, to expand the use of evidence-based approaches to turning around our lowest-performing schools; $92 million for Magnet Schools, which will include a priority for STEM; and increased support for teacher training under an expanded Advanced Placement program that will improve access to other accelerated learning options, such as early-college high schools.

- Giving more students access to 21st century STEM courses and curriculum. Building on the announcements in December 2014 by the Administration and private-sector partners to expand computer-science education in K-12 schools, the 2016 Budget requests more than $60 million for NSF's STEM + Computing Partnerships program, which specifically focuses on support for computer science education with teacher training, new curriculum, and partnership efforts. The 2016 Budget also provides $15 million for the National Institutes of Health (NIH) to invest in the Science Education Partnership Award (SEPA) program, leveraging the expertise of the biomedical research community to support innovative curriculum in K-12 schools, and $4 million for the Environmental Protection Agency (EPA) to invest in environmental education grants. In addition, the Department of Defense (DOD) will invest $3 million in expanding STEM opportunities for children of military families. The DOD investments will build on a multi-year record of success under the National Math and Science Initiative's (NMSI) Initiative for Military Families. In the Initiative, DOD, NMSI, and private-sector investments have helped more than 75 military-connected public high schools prepare more students for college and career by improving access to and successful completion of Advanced Placement (AP) courses, with those schools showing, on average, a 67 percent increase in passing math, science, and English AP scores. DOD will explore additional options to leverage its science and engineering workforce, expertise, and resources to enhance this multiyear record of success in STEM learning for military children.

Recruiting, Preparing, and Supporting Excellent STEM Teachers

- Preparing 100,000 excellent and new STEM teachers over a decade. In his 2011 State of the Union address, the President called for a new effort to prepare 100,000 STEM teachers over the next decade with strong teaching skills and deep content knowledge. Answering the President's call to action, more than 230 organizations formed a coalition called *100Kin10*.[4] These organizations have made over 250 measurable commitments to increase the supply of excellent STEM teachers, including recruiting and preparing more than 43,000 teachers in the first five years of the initiative. In addition, in 2014 ED announced more than $35 million in STEM-focused five-year grants under the Teacher Quality Partnership Grant program. These grants, over a five-year grant period, are expected to total $175 million and will support more than 11,000 new teachers, primarily in STEM fields, in high-need schools. To build on a growing set of public and private investments, ED is proposing $139 million in the 2016 Budget for its new Teacher and Principal Pathways program, $100 million of which would support high-quality teacher preparation with a priority for STEM teacher-preparation programs that recruit and train effective STEM teachers for high-need schools. Finally, the National Science Foundation will continue its more than $60 million-per-year investment in the Robert Noyce Scholarship program to train new STEM teachers.

- Strengthening STEM teaching and learning. To support innovative STEM teaching and the critical role of partnerships, ED's 2016 Budget provides more than $200 million in the Math and Science Partnerships program, a $50 million increase over 2015 enacted levels. This expansion, coupled with targeted program reforms, would build on the previous success of the program in giving educators the ability to engage in innovative STEM teaching. Expanding the program also would allow for better leveraging of local resources and assets to encourage comprehensive STEM education reform. The enhanced program would focus on strategic partnerships of school districts, businesses, universities, museums, Federal agencies, and other educational entities. These partnerships would transform how a district delivers STEM education so that students are: (1) engaged in learning experiences that inspire curiosity; (2) connected to the real-world experiences of STEM professionals; (3)given project-based making and learning experiences; and provided access and support – especially for girls and under-represented minorities – to succeed in rigorous math and science coursework. The expanded Math

---

[4] http://100kin10.org/

and Science Partnership program will also create a national, online community of STEM educators in a STEM Virtual Learning Network.

Investing in Testing and Scaling Effective Models

- <u>Identifying and scaling what works in STEM education.</u> The Budget funds ED's Investing in Innovation (i3) program at $300 million, a $180 million increase over 2015 enacted levels, to develop and test effective practices and provide better information to States and districts on what works in K-12 education, including a priority for strategies that improve student success in STEM subjects. The i3 program has built a strong record in expanding effective STEM programs. For example, one recipient of a Validation grant, the National Math and Science Initiative's College Readiness Program, has helped enroll more than 6,300 students in college-level AP courses in Colorado and Indiana, with the number of passing scores on math, science, and English AP exams increasing in the first year. In Colorado, 246 more students passed their AP exams, an increase of 39 percent, and in Indiana, 448 additional students earned passing scores, a 66 percent increase. Complementary investments in building evidence on effective STEM programs include the Administration's proposal for nearly $92 million to support NSF's Discovery Research K-12, which invests in research on teaching and learning STEM.

- <u>Making the STEM fields more inclusive.</u> NSF is proposing $15 million for a new INCLUDES (Inclusion across the Nation of Communities of Learners that have been Underrepresented for Diversity in Engineering and Science) program that will develop and test strategies and build partnerships to enhance the participation of those who have been traditionally underserved or underrepresented in STEM fields. INCLUDES investments are intended to produce rapid progress on changing the balance of diversity in science and technology, have significant national impact for the participation of underrepresented groups, inspire the community, forge new partnerships, and catalyze new approaches.

Undergraduate STEM Education

The focus of the President's 2016 Budget's undergraduate STEM education investments is on supporting the President's goal to increase the number of well-prepared graduates with STEM degrees by one million over a decade, including investments to:

- <u>Transform undergraduate teaching and learning with NSF investments.</u> The Budget proposes approximately $135 million at NSF, an increase of almost $30 million, for a comprehensive Foundation-wide effort to improve undergraduate STEM education, including steps to improve undergraduate teaching, expand student opportunities to have authentic research experiences, address the high failure rate for introductory mathematics, leverage new technologies, and increase degree completion of women and under-represented minorities in STEM. The Budget also proposes $78 million for NSF's Research Experiences for Undergraduates program to provide early opportunities for college students to conduct research, which can be especially influential in maintaining a student's interest in STEM. The Administration is also proposing over $60 million for NSF's Advanced Technological Education program, which invests in the education of technicians for in-demand high-technology fields, with a focus on partnerships between academic institutions and employers.

- <u>Driving performance and innovation in higher education.</u> ED will make a series of investments to drive performance and improve outcomes in higher education, with the potential to increase the number of students who complete with STEM degrees. This includes: (1) expanding the First in the World fund to $200 million, which will support and test promising institutional innovations and practices that improve educational outcomes in college; (2) a new $200 million Career and Technical Education Innovation Fund to support innovative, evidence-based job training programs in high-demand fields; and (3) creation of a new ED Idea Lab, modeled on the Idea Lab at the Department of Health and Human Services, to bring forward and incubate new ideas from agency staff and external innovators on mission priorities, starting with higher education. The Department of Education will also invest in expanding higher education opportunities for under-represented groups with $100 million in the Hispanic-Serving Institutions STEM and Articulation program, sustained funding for Gaining Early Awareness and Readiness for Undergraduate Programs (GEAR UP), and increased funding for ED's Federal TRIO Programs – a set of programs that have a strong focus on increasing access to STEM education.

Graduate Education

The 2016 Budget's graduate STEM-education investments focus on preparing highly-skilled scientists and engineers who will support American innovation. Key investments to achieve this goal include:

- <u>Enhancing NSF's efforts to train tomorrow's workforce.</u> The Budget provides $400 million at NSF for the Graduate Research Fellowships and Research Traineeship Programs to support thousands of outstanding graduate-student researchers who will be tomorrow's leaders in the innovation economy in a range of careers. In addition, these graduate students will gain valuable knowledge of STEM opportunities in the Federal agencies under the Graduate Research Internships Program, which has a number of Federal agencies as partners. In addition, NSF is supporting $45 million for CyberCorps to help more students meet the growing need for an expanded and capable cybersecurity workforce.

- <u>Investing in a DOE program to prepare graduate students for high-priority STEM fields.</u> The President's 2016 Budget includes $10 million for DOE's Computational Sciences Graduate Fellowship (CSGF) to support training in advanced computing relevant to DOE's high performance computing capabilities and to the challenges of exascale computing.

- <u>Continuing support for major graduate-training programs,</u> including $470 million for the NIH's Ruth L. Kirschstein National Research Service Award Institutional Research Training Grants (T32 and T35 awards only), which provide funding to prepare individuals for careers in the biomedical, behavioral, and social sciences. In addition,

DOD will invest over $90 million in the Science, Mathematics and Research for Transformation Scholarship and the National Defense Science and Engineering Graduate programs to meet key national security workforce needs.

Informal STEM Education

The President believes that many more boys and girls must have access to engaging STEM experiences that show them the potential of these high-wage careers. That is why the President started the tradition of hosting yearly White House Science Fairs to honor STEM achievement, challenged students to be "makers of things," and hosted the first-ever White House Maker Faire last year, led by example as the first President to ever write a line of code as part of "Hour of Code" with students, and called on the Nation's 200,000 Federal scientists and engineers to volunteer in their local communities and think of creative ways to engage students in STEM subjects.

The 2016 Budget builds on the President's leadership with key investments that include:

- Identifying best practices to engage youth in STEM. The Administration proposes $60 million for NSF's Advancing Informal Science Learning program, focusing on the research and model-building contributions of the program to better understand effective means and innovative models for engaging today's young people and adults in science outside of school settings.

- Improving the reach of informal STEM education. The Budget provides $5 million to the Smithsonian Institution to improve the reach of informal STEM education by ensuring that museum materials and other National treasures are accessible to more students and aligned with what students are learning in the classroom. In addition, the Institute of Museum and Library Services (IMLS) will continue to support STEM and "making" programs, with special emphasis on programs targeted for at-risk youth.

- Supporting community-based STEM activities. As part of its 2016 Budget, the Corporation for National and Community Service (CNCS) will continue to implement and expand STEM AmeriCorps, a multi-year initiative to engage AmeriCorps members in mobilizing STEM professionals to inspire young people, including underrepresented students, to excel in science, technology, engineering, and math and build the pipeline for future STEM careers.

- Supporting high-quality STEM education programs at NASA. The Budget supports NASA's efforts to internally restructure and better integrate its STEM education programs to reach more students and teachers, with $89 million for the Office of Education and complementary $20 million provided under NASA's Science Mission Directorate to competitively fund the best applications of NASA Science assets to STEM education goals.

Supporting Innovation and Next-Generation Learning Technologies

Building on the President's *Strategy for American Innovation* and the Administration's commitment to tackle the Grand Challenges of the 21st Century, the Budget provides support for:

- ARPA-ED. $50 million for the Advanced Research Projects Agency for Education (ARPA-ED), a "DARPA for Education." ARPA-ED will allow the Department of Education to advance the field of education research, development, and demonstration by sponsoring rapid-cycle projects aimed at solving vexing problems within modern education. ARPA-ED will enable opportunities to accelerate development of the technology solutions within both the public and private sector; shaping of the next wave of research and development; investment in the development of innovative education technologies, and identification and scaling of the best and most relevant research and development from other Federal agencies.

- Supporting teachers and helping prepare them for the Digital Age. The Budget invests $3 billion to provide broad support for educators at every phase of their careers, from ensuring they have strong preparation before entering the classroom, to pioneering new approaches to help teachers succeed and equip them with the tools and training they need to implement college- and career-ready standards. Recognizing the importance of integrating technology into the classroom, this investment includes $200 million for an improved Education Technology State Grants program focused on providing educators with training and support to maximize the impact of expanded access to technology to provide high-quality, personalized instruction to students, while protecting their privacy. The Budget also supports a companion initiative funded at $1 billion annually for five years in mandatory funding that will support State and local efforts to attract the best candidates to the teaching profession, especially in hard-to-fill positions such as math and science, and prepare them for the demands of the classroom, while also creating a culture of excellence and professional growth for teachers throughout their careers.

- Investing in new methods and new insights from the fields. ED's Institute of Education Sciences will continue its support for a "Virtual Learning Laboratory" initiative, which explores the use of rapid experimentation and "Big Data" to discover better ways to help students master important concepts in core academic subjects such as STEM and looks for opportunities to expand its use of rapid low-cost randomized control trials. In addition, the Budget requests $10 million at ED for school districts and researchers to partner to develop and test "non-cognitive" interventions that contribute to student success, such as academic perseverance, self-control, and social and emotional skills.

Making the Most of Our STEM Investments

The President's 2016 Budget maintains a strong commitment to the goals of the Five-Year Strategic Plan. This means:

- Agencies will coordinate their STEM education investments through implementation of the Federal STEM Education Five-Year Strategic Plan, looking for opportunities to build the evidence base, share what works, and leverage each other's expertise and resources. Agency members of the National Science and Technology Council's Committee on STEM Education (CoSTEM) have convened working groups focused on each of the five priority areas identified in the Five-Year Strategic Plan and are working to coordinate and better align existing programs, develop joint pilot projects, and develop common data-collection strategies.

- Agencies will focus on internal consolidations and eliminations, while funding their most effective programs. As a result, the 2016 Budget continues to reduce fragmentation, building on the substantial number of internal consolidations and eliminations that agencies began implementing in 2013.

- Similar to the Administration's 2015 Budget, the Administration is not requesting a transfer of funding between agencies but instead is ensuring that agencies have enough resources to continue strong interagency coordination. To support these and related activities, the Budget provides support for the work agencies are doing to implement the Five-Year Strategic Plan, with a focus on building and using evidence-based practices and developing new interagency models for leveraging assets and expertise.

II.   Progress on Implementation of the Federal STEM Education 5-Year Strategic Plan

The Federal STEM Education 5-Year Strategic Plan (Strategic Plan),[5] released in May 2013, was the result of substantial work by the Administration to identify strategic priorities for STEM-education investment, ways that agencies could collectively contribute to advance those priorities, and areas where such efforts could grow the evidence base of what works in STEM education.

Many Federal agencies prioritize STEM education and have developed related initiatives that are unique to their respective missions, visions, and resources. Building on these efforts, the Strategic Plan identifies five priority investment areas, each with a corresponding national goal toward which Federal agencies and collaborators in state and local entities and the private sector should aspire:

- Improve STEM teacher training. Prepare 100,000 excellent new K-12 STEM teachers by 2020 and support the existing STEM teacher workforce.

- Increase and sustain youth and public engagement in STEM. Support a 50 percent increase in the number of youth in America who have authentic STEM experiences each year prior to completing high school.

- Enhance STEM experience of undergraduate students. Graduate 1 million additional students with degrees in STEM fields over a decade.

- Better serve groups historically under-represented in STEM fields. Increase the number of underrepresented minorities that graduate with STEM degrees in the next 10 years and improve women's participation in areas of STEM where they are significantly underrepresented.

- Design graduate education for tomorrow's STEM workforce. Provide graduate-trained STEM professionals with foundational expertise in basic research, options to acquire specialized skills in areas of national importance and mission agency's needs, and ancillary skills needed for success in a broad range of careers.

In addition, CoSTEM agencies recognize that improved coordination and collaboration across the Federal STEM-education investment portfolio is necessary to make the most effective use of resources and expertise. Accordingly, the Strategic Plan outlines two priority coordination approaches:

- Build new models for leveraging assets and expertise. Implement a concept of lead and collaborating agencies to leverage capabilities across agencies to ensure the most significant impact of Federal STEM education investments.

---

[5] http://www.whitehouse.gov/sites/default/files/microsites/ostp/stem_stratplan_2013.pdf

- <u>Build and use evidence-based approaches.</u> Conduct STEM education research and evaluation to build evidence about promising practices and program effectiveness, use across agencies, and share with the public to improve the impact of the Federal STEM education investment.

The Strategic Plan laid out draft implementation roadmaps in each of the priority STEM education investment and coordination areas and proposed potential short, medium, and long-term objectives and strategies to help Federal agencies achieve the goals described.

With the release of the Strategic Plan, the CoSTEM directed the Task Force on Federal Coordination in STEM Education (FC-STEM) to undertake planning for Strategic Plan implementation. As of January 2014, FC-STEM continues this implementation role and has been re-chartered as the Subcommittee on Federal Coordination in STEM Education under the CoSTEM. In addition, since the release of the plan, FC-STEM has launched five working groups, each tasked with executing one of the five strategic objectives described above.

These interagency groups have convened over the past year on Strategic Plan implementation. Across priority areas, these working groups are planning new pilot projects that leverage agency assets and expertise to improve the reach of STEM content in formal school and afterschool settings; increasing coordination across agencies to identify meaningful opportunities and experiences for P-12 teachers, undergraduate, and graduate students; identifying localities with common grantees to best leverage Federal investment; and developing common data collection strategies for improved evaluation.

Going forward, CoSTEM and FC-STEM will continue to make progress on Strategic Plan implementation, with particular focus on short- and medium-term implementation goals. The working groups will also incorporate input from the STEM education community and make the adjustments needed to ensure progress on the shared goal of giving more Americans access to critical STEM skills.

Strategic Plan Codified as a Cross Agency Priority Goal

The STEM Education Strategic Plan has also been codified in early 2014 as a Cross Agency Priority Goal (CAP).[6] This step will institutionalize the STEM Education Strategic Plan into agency performance metrics and requires agencies to issue public implementation updates every quarter.

To read the FY 2014 Quarter 2, 3, and 4 reports, see the Appendix.

---

[6] http://www.performance.gov/node/3404?view=public#apg

III. Reducing Fragmentation and Duplication of STEM Education Programs

The Administration has made progress to reduce fragmentation and duplication of STEM education programs. Over the past two years, the overall number of STEM programs has been reduced by 40 percent, and the 2016 Budget continues to reduce fragmentation of STEM education programs across the Government. Compared to the 2015 enacted budget, 20 programs are proposed for elimination and five new programs are proposed.

Similar to the Administration's 2015 Budget proposal, agencies will focus principally on internal consolidations and eliminations to reduce fragmentation and duplication. Also similar to 2015, the Administration is not requesting a transfer of funding between agencies, but instead ensuring that agencies have enough resources to continue strong interagency coordination.

Internal Consolidations

The 2016 Budget maintains the Administration's focus on reducing fragmentation through internal consolidations and eliminations lead by the agencies. Notable examples include:

- Continued consolidation of NASA's education investments, by merging education efforts previously distributed throughout the agency to within the Office of Education. Through a competitive process, the Office will identify and support the most effective STEM education activities across NASA. Additionally, the President's FY16 Budget provides $20 million for NASA's Science Mission Directorate to fund through a competitive process the best applications of NASA's science assets to meet the Nation's STEM goals, as well as $6 million to continue to fund the Global Learning and Observation to Benefit the Environment activity.

- Consolidation of NSF education investments, helping NSF to focus on improving the research base and delivery of undergraduate STEM education. The Budget proposes approximately $135 million at NSF for a comprehensive Foundation-wide effort to improve undergraduate STEM education.

Cross-Agency Partnerships

Under CoSTEM and the STEM Education Strategic Plan, agencies have also begun a number of efforts to reduce duplication through increased coordination and collaboration. These efforts include:

- ED's interagency collaboration to add more STEM education into its $1.2 billion after-school program. ED's 21st Century Community Learning Centers (CCLC) program is the Federal government's largest investment in after-school programming, serving more than 1 million students a year. Announced at the beginning of 2015, CCLC is spearheading three inter-agency collaborations that effectively leverage the STEM education investments of three different Federal agencies. These collaborations are supporting important goals in the STEM Strategic Plan: offering students authentic STEM content and experiences, as well as opportunities to engage with STEM subject-matter experts.

As part of these efforts, over 2015, an existing pilot collaboration with NASA and CCLC will be expanded, and CCLC collaborations with two other Federal agencies – the National Park Service (NPS) and IMLS – will be piloted. The number of participating sites will expand fivefold (from around 20 to over 100); the number of participating agencies will double from two (ED and NASA) to four; and the collaborations will benefit students nationwide. Participating sites represent broad geographic diversity and encompass rural and urban settings.

- o The **NASA** collaboration provides students with the opportunity to solve challenges based on real mission data and experiences that occur during exploration of the solar system. NASA staff will provide face-to-face as well as ongoing online professional development to the CCLC staff. Throughout the program, both staff and students will be provided with several opportunities to interact directly with NASA scientists and engineers as they learn first-hand about engineering design and practices. In 2013, 20 CCLC sites across three states participated in the NASA challenges, offering three different engineering-design challenges; in 2015, up to 80 CCLC sites across 10 states will participate and will have the option of choosing from six engineering challenges.

- o The **NPS** pilot program introduces environmental monitoring and citizen-science programs to students in CCLC programs at schools overseen by the Bureau of Indian Education at 11 sites in five states. Native Americans are the most under-represented group in the STEM fields. These programs are site-based, located in national parks, and focused on introducing students to the natural resources in their region and related science. Working with Hands on the Land, a national network of field classrooms and agency resources that connects students, teachers, families, and volunteers with public lands and waterways, NPS will engage park rangers and other subject-matter experts to provide professional development to CCLC staff at participating sites throughout the program and will provide subject-matter expertise to students.

- o The pilot program with **IMLS** will introduce students at 25 sites across five states to making and tinkering projects – part of a growing "Maker Movement" that is providing a powerful way to get young people interested in STEM. This program will link science museums and science youth-serving programs with CCLC sites. Participating staff will be trained by the Exploratorium, a San Francisco-based science center with a history of innovation in maker education, so they can serve as subject-matter experts, provide training to their colleagues, and work with youth participants.

- <u>NSF establishes interagency-partnerships to give NSF-funded graduate students knowledge of STEM opportunities in the Federal agencies.</u> The Budget provides $400 million at NSF for the Graduate Research Fellowships and Research Traineeship Programs to support thousands of outstanding graduate-student researchers who will lead our Nation's innovation economy through a range of STEM careers. To leverage the STEM expertise and career experiences available across Federal agencies, NSF has developed partnerships with a growing number of agencies, such as EPA, the Smithsonian Institution, and the Office of Naval Research, so that these graduate students will gain valuable knowledge of STEM opportunities across the government and STEM fields under the Graduate Research Internships Program.

- <u>Collaborating as part of multi-sector coalitions.</u> Agencies are also collaborating as part of larger multi-sector coalitions, such as *100Kin10*, a partnership of over 230 organizations working together to meet the President's goal of training 100,000 excellent STEM teachers over the next decade. In addition to private-sector and philanthropic organizations, 100kin10 now includes as members ED, DOE, NASA, NSF, and NOAA.

IV.   Dissemination of Information about Federal STEM Education Resources

Federal agencies, both directly and as part of CoSTEM, communicate via a number of methods to the general public. This includes information for the broader STEM education community about: Federal STEM education resources; improvements to and new collaborations within existing programs; results and best practices from Federally-funded research; and progress on the Federal STEM education 5-Year Strategic Plan. Federal agencies also solicit input on how best to organize future STEM education investments.

A few examples in the past year of disseminating resources include:

- CoSTEM information resources. In Fall 2014, CoSTEM agencies collaborated to release a _STEM Resources for Community Colleges_ webpage,[7] which includes publicly available information regarding resources, relevant reports, funding opportunities, webinars, and more happening across Federal agencies. The webpage will be regularly updated and is designed to reach community college leadership, faculty, and students.

- Agency information resources. Webinar series and online information is posted across Federal agencies to inform the community of Federal grants, programs, and other resources. A list of examples includes:

  - **NSF** utilizes websites and social media, formal publications such as journal articles and reports, and resource centers that support existing grantees and disseminate program findings via websites, conferences, meetings, and workshops to share information specifically about agency investments to broaden the participation and increase the success of women and minority students underrepresented in STEM fields. Via these methods, information on funding opportunities, research and evaluation findings, and best practices is disseminated to existing grantees, new applicants, the academic community, the general public, and communities of practice that focus on research and evaluation of efforts targeting underserved audiences.

  - **NASA** sends an Education EXPRESS weekly email to a distribution list of more than 20,000 subscribers (and amplifies top news to many more followers via social media). These messages contain information from NASA and 16 other Federal agencies about workshops; internships and fellowships; applications for grants or collaborations; promotions for student and educator opportunities; online professional development; and other opportunities. In addition, NASA hosts a digital learning network, distributing more than 40 content modules highlighting NASA missions and objectives to viewers everywhere.

---

[7] http://www2.ed.gov/about/offices/list/ovae/pi/cclo/stem.html

    o **NOAA** hosts webinars to disseminate information on available resources, promote quicker adoption of effective practices, and promote wider participation in Federal funding opportunities.

In addition, CoSTEM has shared a number of resources with the STEM education community to communicate its work on the Strategic Plan and to solicit feedback. This includes:

- Quarterly CAP goal implementation updates. To inform the STEM education community of progress made toward Strategic Plan implementation, quarterly updates on the STEM education CAP goal will be published at **performance.gov**, with CAP goal 2014 Quarter 2, 3, and 4 reports in the Appendix.

- Stakeholder meetings. In April 2014, CoSTEM gathered STEM education community leaders to hear input on how to most effectively implement the Federal STEM Education 5-year Strategic Plan. Working group leads for the five priority areas described their progress to-date and plans for moving forward and heard input from the community as to how Strategic Plan implementation could most effectively improve STEM education delivery and STEM learning for students in communities across the country.

- Undergraduate STEM education reform. As part of the White House College Opportunity Initiative which was highlighted at the December 4 College Opportunity Day of Action hosted by the President, Vice President Biden, and the First Lady, NSF produced and distributed a brief on the CoSTEM undergraduate education priority objectives in the Strategic Plan. This brief included the goals for the undergraduate STEM education work of CoSTEM, evidence-based methods already known to the field, gaps in understanding for improving undergraduate STEM learning, and available resources. Faculty, higher education leadership, and non-profit and philanthropic leaders received this information at STEM education regional meetings held throughout the fall leading up to the Day of Action.

- Dual role of graduate students. In December 2013, OMB published new Uniform Guidance,[8] which included a provision recognizing the dual role of graduate students in Federal awards at 2 CFR 200.400, paragraph (f). The language notes that in applying standard cost principles non-Federal entities that educate and engage students in research, the dual role of students as both trainees and employees must be recognized. In 2 CFR 200.472, the Uniform Guidance further clarifies that the costs of training and education provided for employee development is allowable. Combined, these provisions make clear that students as trainees supported by Federal dollars may use their supported time to engage in professional development opportunities that would promote and expand their skills set and expertise to compete for a variety of careers in the STEM workforce. This guidance is effective for awards made after December 26, 2014.

---

[8] http://www.ecfr.gov/cgi-bin/text-idx?SID=5e1569d0f873cab0ebb4028892493a08&tpl=/ecfrbrowse/Title02/2cfr200_main_02.tpl

Table 1. Federal STEM Education Funding by Agency

Table 1. Federal STEM Education Funding by Agency
(budget authority in millions)

	2014 Enacted	2015 Estimate	**2016 Budget**
Agriculture	89	90	**83**
Commerce	35	35	**22**
Defense	132	142	**117**
Education	507	528	**685**
Energy	49	50	**54**
Health and Human Services	619	616	**601**
Homeland Security	6	5	**5**
Interior	3	3	**3**
Transportation	86	90	**108**
CNCS	14	14	**15**
Environmental Protection Agency	20	19	**9**
NASA	127	164	**121**
National Science Foundation	1,179	1,176	**1, 231**
Nuclear Regulatory Commission	20	16	**1**
Smithsonian Institution	0	0	**5**
Total Federal STEM Education	2,885	2,946	3,059

AGENCY	SUB-AGENCY	PROGRAM	2014 Enacted	2015 Estimate	2016 Budget
Agriculture	NIFA	1890 Facilities Grant Program	19.7	19.7	20.4
Agriculture	NIFA	1890 Institutions Capacity Building Grants Program: Extension	6.4	6.4	6.8
Agriculture	NIFA	1890 Institutions Capacity Building Grants Program: Teaching	6.4	6.4	6.8
Agriculture	NIFA	4-H Science, 4-H Youth Development Program	23.5	23.5	23.5
Agriculture	APHIS	AgDiscovery	0.5	0.8	0.8
Agriculture	NIFA	Agriculture in the Classroom	0.6	0.6	-
Agriculture	NIFA	AITC Secondary Postsecondary Agriculture Education Challenge Grants (SPECA)	0.9	0.9	-
Agriculture	NIFA	Alaska Native-Serving and Native Hawaiian-Serving Institutions Education Competitive Grants Program	3.2	3.2	3.2
Agriculture	NIFA	Hispanic-Serving Institutions Education Grants Program	9.2	9.2	9.2
Agriculture	NIFA	Insular Programs	1.8	2.0	1.8
Agriculture	NIFA	New Era Rural Technology Competitive Grants Program (RTP)	-	-	-
Agriculture	NIFA	NIFA Fellowship Grants Program	7.3	7.5	10.4
Agriculture	NIFA	Women and Minorities in Science, Technology, Engineering and Mathematics Fields Program (WAMS)	0.4	0.4	-
Agriculture	NIFA	Multicultural Scholars, Graduate Fellowship and Institution Challenge Grants	9.0	9.0	-
CNCS	AmeriCorps	CNCS STEM Programs	13.9	13.9	15.3
Commerce	NOAA	Competitive Education Grants (including Environmental Literacy Grants)	3.6	4.0	-
Commerce	NOAA	Dr. Nancy Foster Scholarship Program	0.5	0.5	-
Commerce	NOAA	Educational Partnership Program with Minority Serving Institutions	14.4	14.4	14.4
Commerce	NOAA	Ernest F. Hollings Undergraduate Scholarship Program	5.3	5.4	6.0
Commerce	NOAA	National Sea Grant College Program	1.0	1.0	-
Commerce	NIST	NIST Summer Institute for Middle School Teachers	0.3	0.3	-
Commerce	NOAA	NOAA Bay Watershed Education and Training (B-WET)	7.2	7.2	-
Commerce	NOAA	NOAA Teacher at Sea Program	0.6	0.6	-
Commerce	NIST	STEM Pipeline for the Next Generation Scientists and Engineers.	1.0	1.0	1.0
Commerce	NIST	Summer Undergraduate Research Fellowship (SURF)	0.8	0.8	0.8

AGENCY	SUB-AGENCY	PROGRAM	2014 Enacted	2015 Estimate	2016 Budget
Defense		Army Educational Outreach Program (AEOP)	9.4	9.3	9.4
Defense		Awards to Stimulate and Support Undergraduate Research Experiences (ASSURE)	4.5	4.5	4.5
Defense		DoD STARBASE Program	25.0	25.0	-
Defense		National Defense Education Program (NDEP) Science, Mathematics And Research for Transformation (SMART)	46.3	45.5	49.6
Defense		National Defense Science and Engineering Graduate (NDSEG) Fellowship Program	36.0	36.0	41.4
Defense		Navy - Science and Engineering Apprenticeship Program (SEAP)	1.0	1.0	1.0
Defense		Navy Historically Black Colleges and Universities/Minority Institutions Research and Education Partnership	4.2	3.6	4.0
Defense		SeaPerch	1.1	-	-
Defense	NSA	Stokes Educational Scholarship Program	1.9	1.6	1.6
Defense		The Naval Research Enterprise Intern Program (NREIP)	1.3	1.3	1.3
Defense		University NanoSatellite Program	0.8	0.8	0.8
Defense		National Defense Education Program (NDEP) Military Child STEM Educational	-	13.0	3.0
Education	OPE	Developing Hispanic Serving Institutions STEM and articulation programs	92.8	92.7	100.0
Education	OPE	Graduate Assistance in Areas of National Need (GAANN)	29.3	29.3	29.3
Education	IES	High School Longitudinal Study of 2009	4.7	4.8	4.9
Education	OII	Investing in Innovation	12.0	25.0	40.0
Education	OESE	Mathematics and Science Partnerships/Effective Teaching and Learning for a	149.7	152.7	202.7
Education	OPE	Minority Science and Engineering Improvement Program	9.0	9.0	9.0
Education	IES	Research in Special Education	3.9	9.7	14.1
Education	IES	Research, Development, and Dissemination	38.0	37.0	40.0
Education	OPE	Strengthening Predominantly Black Institutions	5.7	5.7	5.7
Education	OESE	Teacher Incentive Fund	31.5	29.9	28.4
Education	OPE	Teacher Loan Forgiveness	87.0	89.0	93.0
Education	OPE	Upward Bound Math and Science Program	43.1	43.1	43.1
Education	OII	Next Generation High Schools	-	-	75.0

AGENCY	SUB-AGENCY	PROGRAM	2014 Enacted	2015 Estimate	2016 Budget
Energy	Office of Energy Efficiency and Renewable Energy, Vehicle Technologies	Advanced Vehicle Competitions	2.0	2.5	2.5
Energy	Office of Science, Office of Workforce Development for Teachers and Scientists	Community College Internship (formerly Community College Institute of Science and Technology)	0.7	1.0	1.2
Energy	Office of Science, Advanced Scientific Computing Research	Computational Sciences Graduate Fellowship	8.7	3.0	10.0
Energy	Office of Energy Efficiency and Renewable Energy, Vehicle	Graduate Automotive Technology Education	2.3	-	-
Energy	Office of Environmental Management	HBCU Mathematics, Science & Technology, Engineering and Research Workforce Development Program	7.0	8.0	8.0
Energy	Office of Energy Efficiency and Renewable Energy, Advance Manufacturing	Industrial Assessment Centers	5.3	6.0	6.0
Energy	Office of Science, Office of Workforce Development for	National Science Bowl	2.8	2.9	2.9
Energy	Office of Science, Office of Fusion	National Undergraduate Fellowship Program in Plasma Physics and Fusion Energy	-	0.3	-
Energy	Office of Science, High Energy Physics	QuarkNet	0.5	-	-
Energy	Office of Science, Office of Workforce Development for Teachers and Scientists	Science Undergraduate Laboratory Internships	7.8	8.3	9.0
Energy	Office of Energy Efficiency and Renewable Energy, Building Technologies	Solar Decathlon	2.2	3.0	2.5
Energy	Office of Fossil Energy	Special Recuitment Programs/Mickey Leland Fellowship	0.7	0.7	0.7
Energy	Office of Science, Office of Workforce Development for	Visiting Faculty Program (formerly Faculty and Student Teams)	1.3	1.7	1.8
Energy	Office of Energy Efficiency and Renewable Energy, Wind Energy	Wind for Schools	-	0.6	0.6
Energy	Office of Science, High Energy Physics	U.S. Particle Accelerator Training	0.6	0.6	0.6
Energy	Office of Science, Office of Workforce Development for	Graduate Student Research Program	2.0	2.5	2.5
Energy	Office of Environmental Management	Subsurface Remediation and Project Management Traineeship	-	2.0	2.0
Energy	Office of Energy Efficiency and Renewable Energy, Advanced Manufacturing	Wide Bandgap Power Electronics Traineeship	-	2.0	2.0

AGENCY	SUB-AGENCY	PROGRAM	2014 Enacted	2015 Estimate	2016 Budget
Energy	Office of Nuclear Energy	Integrated University Program	5.5	5.0	-
Energy	Office of Nuclear Energy	Radiochemistry Traineeships	-	-	2.0
EPA	ORD	Cooperative Training Partnership in Environmental Sciences Research	0.7	0.1	0.3
EPA	Office of Environmental	Environmental Education Grants	3.3	3.3	4.2
EPA	ORD	Greater Research Opportunities (GRO) Fellowships for Undergraduate	1.8	1.8	-
EPA	Office of Environmental	National Environmental Education and Training Partnership	2.2	2.2	2.7
EPA	ORD	P3-People, Prosperity & the Planet-Award: A National Student Design	2.1	1.7	1.4
EPA	NCER	Science to Achieve Results Graduate Fellowship Program	9.3	9.3	-
EPA	ORD	University of Cincinnati/EPA Research Training Grant	0.6	0.6	0.6
HHS	NIH, NIGMS	Bridges to the Baccalaureate Program	6.2	6.2	6.2
HHS	NIH, NCI	Cancer Education Grants Program	6.6	6.6	6.6
HHS	NIH, NINDS	Diversity Research Education Grants in Neuroscience	1.0	1.0	-
HHS	NIH, Intramural Training	Graduate Program Partnerships	11.7	11.7	11.7
HHS	HRSA	Health Careers Opportunity Program	14.2	14.2	-
HHS	NIH, NIGMS	MARC U-STAR NRSA Program	20.4	20.4	20.4
HHS	NIH, NICHD	Mathematics and Science Cognition and Learning (MSCL) Program	10.1	10.1	10.1
HHS		Medical Research Scholars Program (MRSP)	0.1	0.1	0.1
HHS	NIH, NCI	National Cancer Institute Cancer Education and Career Development Program	17.5	17.5	17.5
HHS	NIH, Intramural Training	Post-baccalaureate Intramural Research Training Award Program	19.8	19.8	19.8
HHS	HRSA	Public Health Traineeship	2.5	-	-
HHS	NIH	Ruth L. Kirschstein National Research Service Award Institutional Research	473.2	473.2	473.2
HHS	NIH	Ruth L. Kirschstein NRSA for Individual Predoctoral Fellows, including Underrepresented Racial/Ethnic Groups,Students from Disadvantaged	3.8	3.8	3.8
HHS	NIH, OD	Science Education Partnership Award	14.6	14.6	14.6
HHS	NIH, NICHD	Short Courses in Population Reseach (Education Programs for Population Research R25)	0.6	0.6	0.6
HHS	NIH, NIGMS	Short Courses on Mathematical, Statistical, and Computational Tools for Studying Biological Systems	1.9	1.9	1.9
HHS	NIH, NIEHS	Short Term Educational Experiences for Research (STEER) in the Environmental	0.5	-	-
HHS	NIH, NHLBI	Short-Term Research Education Program to Increase Diversity in Health-Related Research	4.5	4.4	4.4
HHS	NIH, Intramural Training	Student Intramural Research Training Award Program	5.3	5.3	5.3

AGENCY	SUB-AGENCY	PROGRAM	2014 Enacted	2015 Estimate	2016 Budget
HHS	NIH, NHLBI	Summer Institute for Training in Biostatistics	1.5	1.5	1.5
HHS	NIH, Intramural Training	Undergraduate Scholarship Program for Individuals from Disadvantaged Backgrounds	2.8	2.8	2.8
Homeland Security	DNDO	National Nuclear Forensics Expertise Development Program	6.0	5.0	5.2
Interior	Bureau of Land Management	Conservation and Land Management Internship Program	1.5	1.5	1.5
Interior	USGS	EDMAP	0.5	0.5	0.5
Interior	National Park Service	Geoscientists-in-the-Parks Program	0.7	0.7	0.7
NASA	ARMD	Aeronautics Academy	0.3	-	-
NASA	ARMD	Aeronautics Scholarship	1.7	-	-
NASA	Science Mission Directorate (SMD)	Aqua	0.3	-	-
NASA	Science Mission Directorate (SMD)	Aura	0.3	-	-
NASA	Science Mission Directorate (SMD)	Chandra	0.8	-	-
NASA	Science Mission Directorate (SMD)	GLOBE Program	6.0	6.0	6.0
NASA	SOMD	HEOMD-Goldstone Apple Valley Radio Telescope (GAVRT) Project	0.1	-	-
NASA	ESMD	HEOMD-NASA's Beginning Engineering, Science and Technology (BEST) Students (NBS)	0.4	-	-
NASA	ESMD	HEOMD-University Student Launch Initiative	0.5	-	-
NASA	Science Mission Directorate	HST	2.0	-	-
NASA	Center GRC	LERCIP - Lewis Educational Research Collaborative Internship Project (College)	0.1	-	-
NASA	Science Mission Directorate (SMD)	Mars E/PO Formal Ed	0.3	-	-
NASA	Education Office	MUREP	30.0	32.0	30.0

AGENCY	SUB-AGENCY	PROGRAM	2014 Enacted	2015 Estimate	2016 Budget
NASA	SOMD	Reduced Gravity Student Flight Opportunity Project	0.4	-	-
NASA	Science Mission Directorate (SMD)	SOFIA (Stratospheric Observatory for Infrared Astronomy) Education and Public Outreach	0.5	-	-
NASA	Education Office	Space Grant - National Space Grant College and Fellowship Program	40.0	40.0	24.0
NASA	OCT-ST	Space Technology Research Fellowships	15.0	15.0	15.0
NASA	Education Office	STEM Education & Accountability Project	28.6	29.0	25.9
NASA	Science Mission Directorate (SMD)	NASA Science Mission Directorate STEM Projects	-	42.0	20.0
NRC	Office of the Chief Human Capital	Grants to Universities (Curriculum Development) Program	1.8	5.0	-
NRC	Office of the Chief Human Capital Officer	Integrated University Program	15.0	10.0	-
NRC	Small Business and Civil Rights Office	Minority Serving Institutions Program (MSIP)	3.5	0.9	0.7
NSF	Directorate for Education and Human Resources (EHR)	Advanced Informal STEM Learning (AISL), formerly Informal Science Education (ISE)	55.0	55.0	60.0
NSF	Directorate for Education and Human Resources (EHR)	Advanced Technological Education (ATE)	64.0	66.0	66.0
NSF	Directorate for Education and Human Resources (EHR)	Alliances for Graduate Education and the Professoriate (AGEP)	7.8	8.0	8.0
NSF	Directorate for Education and Human Resources (EHR)	Discovery Research K-12 (DR-K12)	91.9	83.8	91.9
NSF	Office of International Science and Engineering (OISE)	East Asia & Pacific Summer Institutes for U.S. Graduate Students (EAPSI)	2.4	2.4	2.4
NSF	Directorate for Math and Physical Sciences (MPS)	Enhancing the Mathematical Sciences Workforce in the 21st Century (EMSW21)	10.0	5.7	-
NSF	Directorate for Education and Human Resources (EHR)	Excellence Awards in Science and Engineering (EASE)	5.8	5.8	5.8
NSF	Directorate for Education and Human Resources (EHR)	Cybercorps: Scholarship for Service (SFS)	45.0	45.0	45.0
NSF	Directorate for Education and Human Resources (EHR) & Office	Graduate Research Fellowship Program (GRFP)	300.0	333.4	337.5

AGENCY	SUB-AGENCY	PROGRAM	2014 Enacted	2015 Estimate	2016 Budget
NSF	Directorate for Education and Human Resources (EHR)	Historically Black Colleges and Universities Undergraduate Program (HBCU-UP)	31.9	32.0	32.0
NSF	Directorate for Education and Human Resources (EHR)	Innovative Technology Experiences for Students and Teachers (ITEST)	25.0	25.0	25.0
NSF	Office of International Science and Engineering (OISE)	International Research Experiences for Students (IRES)	2.3	2.3	2.3
NSF	Directorate for Education and Human Resources (EHR)	Louis Stokes Alliances for Minority Participation (LSAMP)	45.6	46.0	46.0
NSF	NSF	NSF Research Traineeships (NRT)	55.1	61.6	62.0
NSF	Directorate for Education and Human Resources (EHR)	NSF Scholarships in Science, Technology, Engineering, and Mathematics (S-STEM)	75.0	75.0	75.0
NSF	Directorate for Engineering (ENG) and Directorate for Computer &	Research Experiences for Teachers (RET) in Engineering and Computer Science	5.5	6.0	6.1
NSF	Directorate for Education and Human Resources (EHR)	Research Experiences for Undergraduates (REU)	75.2	73.2	77.6
NSF	Directorate for Education and Human Resources (EHR)	Research on Education and Learning (REAL), formerly Research and Evaluation on Education in Science and Engineering (REESE)	48.7	-	-
NSF	Directorate for Education and Human Resources (EHR)	Robert Noyce Scholarship (Noyce) Program	60.9	60.9	60.9
NSF	Directorate for Education and Human Resources (EHR) and Directorate for Computer &	STEM+C Partnerships	69.1	69.6	64.4
NSF	Directorate for Education and Human Resources (EHR)	Tribal Colleges and Universities Program (TCUP)	13.5	13.5	13.5
NSF	Directorate for Education and Human Resources (EHR)	Improving Undergraduate STEM Education (IUSE)	89.0	105.4	134.6
NSF		Inclusion across the Nation of Communities of Learners that have been Underrepresented for Diversity in Engineering and Science (INCLUDES)	-	-	15.0
Smithsonian		STEM Informal Education and Instruction	-	-	5.0
Transportation	Federal Aviation Administration (FAA)	Air Transportation Centers of Excellence	13.0	13.0	18.0
Transportation	Federal Highway Administration (FHWA)	Garrett A. Morgan Technology and Transportation Education Program	0.4	0.4	0.4
Transportation	Federal Highway Administration (FHWA)	National Summer Transportation Institute Program (STI)	2.6	2.8	2.8

AGENCY	SUB-AGENCY	PROGRAM	2014 Enacted	2015 Estimate	2016 Budget
Transportation	Office of the Secretary	Summer Transportation Institute Program for Diverse Groups (STIPDG)	1.2	1.3	1.3
Transportation	Office of the Secretary	University Transportation Centers Program	68.7	72.5	82.0
Transportation	Federal Railroad Administration	Rail-based University Transportation Centers Program	-	-	3.0
Total, All Programs			**2,884.7**	**2,946.1**	**3,059.1**

Note: NASA programs that show zero funding may be eligible to compete for Office of Education funds. Additionally, as part of NASA Science Mission Directorate's (SMD) restructured education program, NASA is moving away from mission-based education projects and towards aggregating efforts into science-based disciplines aligned with SMD divisions.

Cross Agency Priority Goal
Quarterly Progress Update

STEM Education

Goal leaders: Jo Handelsman, Associate Director for Science, White House Office of Science and Technology Policy

Joan Ferrini-Mundy; Assistant Director, National Science Foundation, Education and Human Resources

FY2014 Quarterly Updates

Overview

Goal Statement

Improve science, technology, engineering, and mathematics (STEM) education by implementing the *Federal STEM Education 5-Year Strategic Plan*, announced in May 2013, specifically:

- Improve STEM instruction
- Increase and sustain youth and public engagement in STEM
- Enhance STEM experience of undergraduate students
- Better serve groups historically under-represented in STEM fields
- Design graduate education for tomorrow's STEM workforce
- Build new models for leveraging assets and expertise
- Build and use evidence-based approaches

Urgency

- Advances in STEM have long been central to our Nation's economy, security, and ability to preserve the health of its people and the environment; enhancing U.S. students' engagement and success in STEM disciplines is essential to the United States maintaining its preeminent position in the world.
- We have considerable progress to make given that our K-12 system ranks "middle of the pack" in international comparisons.
- Meeting the growing demand for STEM expertise and competency is important to the economy and our democracy.
- Increasing opportunities in STEM for more Americans is critical to building a just and inclusive society.

Vision

- The Federal STEM Education 5-Year Strategic Plan sets out ambitious national goals to drive Federal investment in five priority STEM education areas toward which significant progress will require improved coherence and coordination across Federal agencies with STEM assets and expertise and STEM education resources.

Progress Update

Federal Coordination in STEM Education (FC-STEM) updates:

- FC-STEM finalized charters for the five Inter-agency Working Groups (IWGS).
- Lead and Co-lead agencies finalized for Inter-agency Working Groups.
- All five IWGS holding regular meetings.
- Agreement that FC STEM will address the coordination objectives as a committee of the whole.
- New NASA co-chair of FC STEM identified.

Collaborations and consideration examples:

- Internal agency-level consolidations:
  - Consolidation of NSF's education investments in undergraduate education within a coherent framework, including release of two solicitations for Improving Undergraduate STEM Education across directorates.
  - Continuing implementation of NASA's education investments through the Office of Education's STEM Education and Accountability Projects (SEAP) program
- Cross-agency partnership examples:
  - Use of *Common Guidelines for Education Research and Development* by NSF and the Institute of Education Sciences at the Department of Education in solicitations
  - Establishment of the Graduate Research Internship Program (GRIP), which expands opportunities for NSF Graduate Research Fellows to enhance their professional development by engaging in mission-related research experiences with partner agencies across the Federal government.

Meetings and Outreach

- IWG co-chairs participated in a milestone and metric workshop facilitated by the Performance Improvement Council (August 2014).
- CoSTEM received a briefing on the progress towards implementation of the 5-year Strategic Plan (October 2014).
- OMB and the CAP Goal team met to review progress of the goal and to discuss key initiatives for the next year (October 2014).
- All of the IWGs met jointly to discuss accomplishments form each group, share challenges, and make recommendations for better integration of cross-IWG work.

Action Plan Summary

	Sub-goal	Major Strategies to Achieve Impact	Key indicators
1.	Improve STEM instruction	• Support teacher preparation efforts that encourage use of evidence-based STEM learning opportunities • Increase and improve authentic STEM experiences for teachers	•Percentage of high school mathematics and science teachers who hold degrees in their teaching field or in science of mathematics education •Number of STEM bachelor's degrees earned annually •Percentage of bachelor's degrees awarded to women, black or African American, Hispanic, and American Indian or Alaska Native students (Plus further indicators in development – see slide 12)
2.	Increase and sustain youth and public engagement in STEM	• Provide access to scientific and engineering assets of the federal government • Integrate STEM into school-readiness and after-school programs • Improve empirical understanding of how authentic STEM experiences influence learning or interest	
3.	Enhance STEM experience of undergraduate students	• Implement evidence-based instructional practices and innovations • Improve STEM education at 2-year colleges and transfer to 4-year colleges • Support the development of university-industry partnerships to provide relevant and authentic experiences • Address high failure rates in introductory undergraduate mathematics	
4.	Better serve groups historically under-represented in STEM fields	• Be more responsive to rapidly changing demographics • Focus investments on developing and testing strategies for improving preparation for higher education • Invest in efforts to create campus climates that are effective in improving success for students from under-represented groups	
5.	Design graduate education for tomorrow's STEM workforce	• Recognize and provide financial support to students of high potential • Provide opportunities for fellows' preparation in areas critical to the Nation • Combine and enhance mechanisms that evaluate the impact of fellowships to inform future federal investments	
6.	Build new models for leveraging assets and expertise	• Collaborate to build implementation roadmaps in the goal areas • Reduce administrative barriers to collaboration • Develop a framework to guide coordinated CoSTEM agency budget requests	
7.	Build and use evidence-based approaches	• Support syntheses of existing research on critical issues in STEM priority areas • Improve and align evaluation and research strategies across federal agencies • Streamline processes for interagency collaboration	

STEM Education Goal Team and Governance Plan

**Oversight and Project Management of
Implementation Working Groups
Goal Leaders:** Joan Ferrini-Mundy and Jo Handelsman
Deputy Goal Leaders: NSF and OSTP

P-12 STEM Instruction

Co-Leads:
- Department of Education
- NSF

Engagement

Co-Leads:
- Smithsonian
- NASA

Undergraduate STEM Education

Co-Leads:
- NSF
- Department of Defense

Under-represented Groups

Co-Leads:
- NSF
- NIH

Graduate Education

Co-Leads:
- NSF
- NIH

Coordination Objectives

Lead:
- FC-STEM

Governance

- Co-STEM: Jo Handelsman (OSTP) and France Córdova (NSF) are Co-Chairs. Annual report from FC-STEM to Co-STEM

- FC-STEM: Joan Ferrini-Mundy (NSF) and Donald James (NASA) are Co-Chairs. Quarterly reports from Inter-agency Working Groups to FC-STEM

5

Q4 Update -Work Plan: Governance and Coordination

- Build new models for leveraging assets and expertise.
- Build and use evidence based approaches.

Barriers/Challenges
- Working groups are at varying stages of development of goal priorities, indicators, and milestones.
- Coordination of goals among IWGs needs to be strengthened.
- Baseline data are not easily available for several key areas.
- There is changing participation in the IWGs.
- External input from stakeholders outside the government is needed.

Key Milestones	Milestone Due Date	Milestone Status	Owner	Anticipated Barriers or Other Issues Related to Milestone Completion
Processes for reporting out to Co-STEM and OMB established	05/2014	Complete	FC-STEM	No barriers identified.
Working groups finalized for each sub-goal, including executive secretary	06/2014	Missed	FC-STEM	NSF co-lead for PK-12 IWG has been identified and will be announced as soon as appointment to the agency is finalized.
Identify baseline data, when appropriate, using relevant data sources	08/2014	Complete	FC-STEM	Baseline data may not always be available or costly to develop.
Evaluate best practices for sharing and coordinating products of working groups	08/2014	Complete	FC-STEM	No barriers identified.
Identify and support opportunities for collaboration across working groups	12/2014	On track	FC-STEM	No barriers identified.

6

Q4 Update - Work Plan: Governance and Coordination

Key Milestones	Milestone Due Date	Milestone Status	Owner	Anticipated Barriers or Other Issues Related to Milestone Completion
Key milestones/metrics/indicators established for all sub-goals	01/2015*	On track	FC-STEM	A potential obstacle may be the lack of regularly collected metrics. A joint meeting of all co-leads to develop milestones was held in August and discussed in October at an FC-STEM meeting.
Simplification of key processes such as development of MOUs to encourage common procedures and collaborations	03/2015	On track	FC-STEM	No barriers identified.

*Due date revised. The original due date was 08/2014. The interagency working groups required more time to develop milestones for each sub-goal.

7

Q4 Update - Work Plan Sub-goal 1: P-12 STEM Education

- Support teacher preparation efforts that encourage use of evidence-based STEM learning opportunities
- Increase authentic STEM experiences for teachers

Key Milestones (Lead: Department of Education / NSF)	Milestone Due Date	Milestone Status	Owner	Anticipated Barriers or Other Issues Related to Milestone Completion
Conduct an initial analysis of teacher internship, fellowship, and scholarship programs supported by CoSTEM agencies	01/2014	Complete	IWG P-12	No barriers identified.
Create a map of physical STEM assets managed by CoSTEM agencies to provide guidance for coordinated regional efforts to improve STEM instruction	01/2014	Complete	IWG P-12	No barriers identified.
Launch STEM-focused teacher training grant competition to grow pathways for effective STEM educators	05/2014	Complete	Department of Education	No barriers identified.
Identify opportunities to leverage related efforts of IWG on Undergraduate Education	12/2014	On track	IWG P-12, IWG Undergrad	Potential obstacles include range of purposes motivating agency commitment to undergraduate and P-12 education, including preservice teacher prep and authentic research experiences for teachers/undergrads.
Create a repository of best practices and research related to teacher preparation and professional learning	02/2015*	On track	IWG P-12	Potential obstacles include range of efforts from various agencies to engage teachers in professional development and limited programs that directly support teacher preparation.

*Due date revised. The original due date was 09/2014. NSF is working with possible Congressional report language along this line.

8

Q4 Update - Work Plan Sub-goal 1: P-12 STEM Education

- Support teacher preparation efforts that encourage use of evidence-based STEM learning opportunities
- Increase authentic STEM experiences for teachers

Key Milestones (Lead: Department of Education / TBD)	Milestone Due Date	Milestone Status	Owner	Anticipated Barriers or Other Issues Related to Milestone Completion
Conduct an in-depth analysis of one regional "hotspot zone" to identify all relevant federal asset activity, programs, and local non-governmental efforts to improve STEM instruction	02/2015*	On track	IWG P-12	Initial analysis has been limited in scope to three areas: Hunstsville, AL; Minneapolis, MN; and, Baltimore area, MD. Limitations may include agency presence in selected areas.

*Due date revised. The original due date was 11/2014. Identifying all federal activities has been more challenging for some agencies than originally anticipated.

Q4 Update - Work Plan Sub-goal 2: Engagement in STEM Education

- Access to scientific and engineering assets of the Federal Government
- Integration of STEM into school readiness and after-school programs
- Empirical understanding of how STEM experiences influence learning

Key Milestones (Lead: Smithsonian Institute / NASA)	Milestone Due Date	Milestone Status	Owner	Anticipated Barriers or Other Issues Related to Milestone Completion
Identify exemplar scientific and engineering assets that feature evaluation to serve as models for STEM Engagement activities	12/2013	Complete	IWG-Engagement	No barriers identified.
Identify audiences that should receive STEM Engagement resources and programs	02/2014	Complete	IWG-Engagement	No barriers identified.
Identify STEM Engagement Activities of CoSTEM agencies	12/2014*	On track	IWG-Engagement	No barriers identified.
Identify evaluation models used to effectively study engagement	01/2015**	On track	IWG-Engagement	No barriers identified.
Implementation of agency commitments related to Making and student engagement announced by President Obama at the White House Maker Faire	06/2015	On track	OSTP	No barriers identified.

*Due date revised. The original due date was 07/2014. The IWG met only occasionally until July 2014 when a co-chair was added, although it was possible to accomplish some collection of materials prior to that.
**Due date revised. The original due date was 09/2014. The IWG did not start meeting until July

Q4 Update - Work Plan Sub-goal 3: Undergraduate STEM Education

- Implementation of evidence-based instructional practices and innovations
- Improve STEM education at 2-year colleges and transfer to 4-year colleges
- Support the development of university-industry partnerships to provide relevant and authentic experiences
- Address high failure rates in introductory mathematics at undergraduate

Key Milestones (Lead: NSF/TBD)	Milestone Due Date	Milestone Status	Owner	Anticipated Barriers or Other Issues Related to Milestone Completion
Share evaluation approaches for undergraduate authentic STEM experiences, including mentoring evaluation instruments	08/2014	Complete	IWG Undergrad	No barriers identified.
Develop shared resource on research-base on undergraduate authentic science experiences	09/2014	Complete	IWG Undergrad	No barriers identified.
Compile agency resources that could be useful to Engineering Deans who signed on to the NAE Grand Challenges effort	09/2014	Complete	IWG Undergrad	No barriers identified.
Leverage related efforts of IWG on Graduate Education	12/2014	On track	IWG Undergrad	No barriers identified.
Identify opportunities to leverage related efforts of IWG on P-12 Education	12/2014	On track	IWG Undergrad	Potential obstacles include range of purposes motivating agency commitment to undergraduate and P-12 education, including preservice teacher education.
Develop an online, cross-agency resource of Federal programs of interest to community colleges	12/2014	Complete	IWG Undergrad	No barriers identified.

11

Q4 Update - Work Plan Sub-goal 3: Undergraduate STEM Education

- Implementation of evidence-based instructional practices and innovations
- Improve STEM education at 2-year colleges and transfer to 4-year colleges
- Support the development of university-industry partnerships to provide relevant and authentic experiences
- Address high failure rates in introductory mathematics at undergraduate

Key Milestones (Lead: NSF/TBD)	Milestone Due Date	Milestone Status	Owner	Anticipated Barriers or Other Issues Related to Milestone Completion
Identify common evaluation elements for undergraduate authentic STEM experiences to be used across federal agencies	10/2015	On track	IWG Undergrad	Potential obstacles include range of purposes motivating agency commitment to undergraduate research and intern opportunities.
Include item on undergraduate mathematics instruction in 2009 High School Longitudinal Survey second follow up:				
A) Decision to do in-depth cognitive testing or field testing on new item for the High School Longitudinal Study on undergraduate mathematics instruction	12/2014 (A)	On track	IWG Undergrad	No barriers identified.
B) Item integrated into HSLS Second Follow-up	4/2015 (B)	On track	IWG Undergrad	Dependent on A
C) Survey data collected from HSLS	12/2016 (C)	On track	IWG Undergrad	Dependent on B
D) Survey results available	12/2017 (D)	On track	IWG Undergrad	Dependent on C

12

30

Q4 Update - Work Plan Sub-goal 4: Broadening Participation in STEM Fields

- Be more responsive to rapidly changing demographics
- Focus investments
- Invest in efforts to create campus climates that are effective in improving success for students from underrepresented groups

Key Milestones (Lead: NIH/NSF)	Milestone Due Date	Milestone Status	Owner	Anticipated Barriers or Other Issues Related to Milestone Completion
Create a repository for reports, literature, and committee products and deliverables for subgroups assigned to each major action item.	12/2014	On track	IWG Co-leads	New milestones created to help facilitate committee work
Conduct a review of existing portfolio of BP efforts (federal)and non-federal models and approaches using the FC STEM inventory, presentations, literature reviews, and reports.	6/2015	On track	IWG BP	After two meetings, it is clear that the committee needs to gain a better understanding of federal portfolio, as well as reports and literature on practices and challenges.
Meet with leads for UG, Graduate, K12, and Engagement IWGs to identify opportunities for collaboration and leveraging of efforts.	2/2015	On track	IWG BP	No barriers identified.
Develop a summary document which includes best practices, challenges, and needs in BP to support strategies and recommendations designed to focus federal BP investments.	6/2015	On track	IWG BP	No barriers identified.
Ideas proposed to maximize the impact of the federal investment with a timeline for agency adoption	12/2015*	On track	IWG BP	No barriers identified.

*Due date revised. The original due date was 10/2014. The IWG held its first meeting in August 2014.

13

Q4 Update - Work Plan Sub-goal 4: Broadening Participation in STEM Fields

- Be more responsive to rapidly changing demographics
- Focus investments
- Invest in efforts to create campus climates that are effective in improving success for students from underrepresented groups

Key Milestones (Lead: NIH/NSF)	Milestone Due Date	Milestone Status	Owner	Anticipated Barriers or Other Issues Related to Milestone Completion
Agencies identify and begin implementation of modifications to existing program portfolio to address gaps to provide more opportunities for URMs in STEM.	9/2015*	On track	IWG BP	No barriers identified.
Agencies identify strategies and timeline for incorporating campus climate guidelines and best practices into funding opportunities	10/2015**	On track	IWG BP	No barriers identified.

*Due date revised. The original due date was 01/2015. The IWG held its first meeting in August 2014 and needs time to review existing research, programs, and exemplary models both within and outside of the federal government to help identify gaps and make recommendations for enhancements.
**Due date revised. The original due date was 06/2015. The IWG held its first meeting in August 2014 and needs more time to complete this milestone.

14

31

Q4 Update - Work Plan Sub-goal 5: Graduate STEM Education

- Recognize and provide financial support to students of high potential
- Provide opportunities for fellows' preparation in areas critical to the Nation
- Combine and enhance mechanisms that evaluate the impact of fellowships to inform future federal investments

Key Milestones (Lead: NSF/NIH)	Milestone Due Date	Milestone Status	Owner	Anticipated Barriers or Other Issues Related to Milestone Completion
Establish MOUs across agencies to broaden research opportunities of NSF fellows	10/2014	Complete	IWG Grad	No barriers identified.
Assemble inventory of evaluation approaches for graduate programs	01/2015	Complete	IWG Grad	No barriers identified.
Identify available resources for the evaluation of graduate programs	01/2015	On track	IWG Grad	No barriers identified.
Identify options such as courses and internships to enhance the quality of graduate training to better address the needs of a future STEM workforce	01/2015	On track	IWG Grad	No barriers identified.
Create common portal for fellowship and traineeship opportunities for graduate students	03/2015*	On track	IWG Grad	No barriers identified.
Expand MOU partners to include most CoSTEM partners in opportunities for NSF fellows	12/2015	On track	IWG Grad	No barriers identified.
Expand Portal to include undergraduate research opportunities	12/2015	On track	IWG Grad and IWG Undergrad	No barriers identified.

*Due date revised. The original due date was 02/2015. Additional time is needed for design of the portal.

15

Q3 Update - Work Plan: Governance and Coordination

- Build new models for leveraging assets and expertise.
- Build and use evidence based approaches.

Barriers/Challenges
- Working groups are at varying stages of development of goal priorities, indicators, and milestones.
- FC-STEM is actively working on strengthening coordination among the working groups.
- Baseline data not easily available for several key areas.

Key Milestones	Milestone Due Date	Milestone Status	Owner	Anticipated Barriers or Other Issues Related to Milestone Completion
Processes for working groups reporting out to Co-STEM established	05/2014	Complete	FC-STEM	No barriers identified.
Working groups finalized for each sub-goal, including executive secretary	06/2014	Missed	FC-STEM	FC-STEM is identifying appropriate co-lead agencies for the remaining two working groups and an FC-STEM executive secretary.
Key milestones/metrics/indicators established for all sub-goals	08/2014	On track	FC-STEM	A potential obstacle may be the lack of regularly collected metrics. A joint meeting of all co-leads to develop milestones will be held in August
Identify baseline data, when appropriate, using relevant data sources	08/2014	On track	FC-STEM	Baseline data may not always be available or costly to develop.
Evaluate best practices for sharing and coordinating products of working groups	08/2014	On track	FC-STEM	No barriers identified. Increased coordination will be discussed at the joint August meeting.
Identify and support opportunities for collaboration across working groups	12/2014	On track	FC-STEM	No barriers identified.
Simplification of key processes such as development of MOU's to encourage common procedures and collaborations	03/2015	On track	FC-STEM	No barriers identified.

16

Q3 Update - Work Plan Sub-goal 1: P-12 STEM Education

- Support teacher preparation efforts that encourage use of evidence-based STEM learning opportunities
- Increase authentic STEM experiences for teachers

Key Milestones (Lead: Department of Education / TBD)	Milestone Due Date	Milestone Status	Owner	Anticipated Barriers or Other Issues Related to Milestone Completion
Conduct an initial analysis of teacher internship, fellowship, and scholarship programs supported by CoSTEM agencies	01/2014	Complete	IWG P-12	No barriers identified.
Create a map of physical STEM assets managed by CoSTEM agencies to provide guidance for coordinated regional efforts to improve STEM instruction	01/2014	Complete	IWG P-12	No barriers identified.
Launch STEM-focused teacher training grant competition to grow pathways for effective STEM educators	05/2014	Complete	Department of Education	No barriers identified.
Key milestones/metrics/indicators established for all sub-goals	08/2014	On track	IWG P-12	No barriers identified
Create a repository of best practices and research related to teacher preparation and professional learning	09/2014	On track	IWG P-12	No barriers identified.
Conduct an in-depth analysis of one regional "hotspot zone" to identify all relevant federal asset activity, programs, and local non-governmental efforts to improve STEM instruction	11/2014	On track	IWG P-12	No barriers identified.

17

Q3 Update - Work Plan Sub-goal 2: Engagement in STEM Education

- Access to scientific and engineering assets of the Federal Government
- Integration of STEM into school readiness and after-school programs
- Empirical understanding of how STEM experiences influence learning

Key Milestones (Lead: Smithsonian Institute / NASA)	Milestone Due Date	Milestone Status	Owner	Anticipated Barriers or Other Issues Related to Milestone Completion
Identify exemplar scientific and engineering assets that feature evaluation to serve as models for STEM Engagement activities	12/2013	Complete	IWG-Engagement	No barriers identified.
Identify audiences that should receive STEM Engagement resources and programs	02/2014	Complete	IWG-Engagement	No barriers identified.
Identify STEM Engagement Activities of CoSTEM agencies	07/2014	On track	IWG-Engagement	No barriers identified.
Identify evaluation models used to effectively study engagement	09/2014	On track	IWG-Engagement	No barriers identified.
Implementation of agency commitments related to Making and student engagement announced by President Obama at the White House Maker Faire	06/2015	On track	OSTP and relevant agencies	No barriers identified.

18

Q3 Update - Work Plan Sub-goal 3: Undergraduate STEM Education

- Implementation of evidence-based instructional practices and innovations
- Improve STEM education at 2-year colleges and transfer to 4-year colleges
- Support the development of university-industry partnerships to provide relevant and authentic experiences
- Address high failure rates in introductory mathematics at undergraduate

Key Milestones (Lead: NSF/TBD)	Milestone Due Date	Milestone Status	Owner	Anticipated Barriers or Other Issues Related to Milestone Completion
Develop shared resource or research-base on undergraduate authentic STEM experiences	09/2014	Complete	IWG Undergrad	No barriers identified.
Share evaluation approaches for undergraduate authentic STEM experiences, including mentoring evaluation instruments	08/2014	On track	IWG Undergrad	No barriers identified.
Compile agency resources that could be useful to Engineering Deans who signed on to the NAE Grand Challenges effort	09/2014	On track	IWG Undergrad	No barriers identified.
Identify opportunities to leverage related efforts of IWG on Graduate Education	12/2014	On track	IWG Undergrad	No barriers identified.
Identify common evaluation elements for undergraduate authentic STEM experiences to be used across federal agencies	10/2015	On track	IWG Undergrad	Potential obstacles include range of purposes motivating agency commitment to undergraduate research and intern opportunities.

19

Q3 Update - Work Plan Sub-goal 4: Broadening Participation in STEM Fields

- Be more responsive to rapidly changing demographics
- Focus investments
- Invest in efforts to create campus climates that are effective in improving success for students from underrepresented groups

Key Milestones (Lead: NIH/NSF)	Milestone Due Date	Milestone Status	Owner	Anticipated Barriers or Other Issues Related to Milestone Completion
Ideas proposed to maximize the impact of the federal investment with a timeline for agency adoption	10/2014	On track	IWG BP	No barriers identified.
Agencies identify and begin implementation of modifications to existing program portfolio to address gaps to provide more opportunities for URMs in STEM	01/2015	On track	IWG BP	No barriers identified.
Agencies identify strategies and timeline for incorporating campus climate guidelines and best practices into funding opportunities	06/2015	On track	IWG BP	No barriers identified.

20

Q3 Update - Work Plan Sub-goal 5: Graduate STEM Education

- Recognize and provide financial support to students of high potential
- Provide opportunities for fellows' preparation in areas critical to the Nation
- Combine and enhance mechanisms that evaluate the impact of fellowships to inform future federal investments

Key Milestones (Lead: NSF/NIH)	Milestone Due Date	Milestone Status	Owner	Anticipated Barriers or Other Issues Related to Milestone Completion
Establish MOUs across agencies to broaden research opportunities of NSF fellows	10/2014	On track	IWG Grad	No barriers identified.
Assemble inventory of evaluation approaches for graduate programs	01/2015	On track	IWG Grad	No barriers identified.
Identify available resources for the evaluation of graduate programs	01/2015	On track	IWG Grad	No barriers identified.
Identify options such as courses and internships to enhance the quality of graduate training to better address the needs of a future STEM workforce	01/2015	On track	IWG Grad	No barriers identified.
Create common portal for fellowship and traineeship opportunities for graduate students	02/2015	On track	IWG Grad	No barriers identified.

21

Q2 Update - Work Plan: Governance and Coordination

Purpose
- To coordinate activity among all sub-goals to implement the Co-STEM strategic plan

Barriers/Challenges
- Working groups are at varying stages of development of goal priorities, indicators, and milestones.
- Coordination of goals among IWGs needs to be strengthened.
- Baseline data not available for several key areas.

Key Milestones	Milestone Due Date	Milestone Status	Last Quarter	Owner	Anticipated Barriers or Other Issues Related to Milestone Completion
Working groups finalized for each sub-goal, including executive secretary	06/2014	On track	N/A	FC-STEM	No barriers identified
Processes for reporting out to Co-STEM and OMB established	05/2014	On track	N/A	FC-STEM	No barriers identified
Key milestones/metrics/indicators established for all sub-goals	08/2014	On track	N/A	FC-STEM	A potential obstacle may be the lack of regularly collected metrics.
Identify baseline data, when appropriate, using relevant data sources	08/2014	On track	N/A	FC-STEM	Baseline data may not always be available.
Evaluate best practices for sharing and coordinating products of working groups	08/2014	On track	N/A	FC-STEM	No barriers identified

22

Q2 Update - Work Plan Sub-goal 1: P-12 STEM Education

- Support teacher preparation efforts that encourage use of evidence-based STEM learning opportunities
- Increase authentic STEM experiences for teachers

Key Milestones (Lead: Department of Education / TBD)	Milestone Due Date	Milestone Status	Last Quarter	Owner	Anticipated Barriers or Other Issues Related to Milestone Completion
Conduct an initial analysis of teacher internship, fellowship, and scholarship programs supported by CoSTEM agencies	01/2014	Complete	N/A	IWG P-12	No barriers identified
Create a map of physical STEM assets managed by CoSTEM agencies to provide guidance for coordinated regional efforts to improve STEM instruction	01/2014	Complete	N/A	IWG P-12	No barriers identified
Launch Stem-focused teacher training grant competition to grow pathways for effective STEM educators.	05/2014	Complete	N/A	Department of Education	
Key milestones/metrics/indicators established for all sub-goals	08/2014	In progress	N/A	IWG P-12	No barriers identified
Create a repository of best practices and research related to teacher preparation and professional learning	09/2014	In progress	N/A	IWG P-12	No barriers identified
Conduct an in-depth analysis of one regional "hotspot zone" to identify all relevant federal asset activity, programs, and local non-governmental efforts to improve STEM instruction	11/2014	Will begin summer 2014	N/A	IWG P-12	No barriers identified

23

Q2 Update - Work Plan Sub-goal 2: Engagement in STEM Education

- Access to scientific and engineering assets of the Federal Government
- Integration of STEM into school readiness and after-school programs
- Empirical understanding of how STEM experiences influence learning

Key Milestones (Lead: Smithsonian Institute / NASA)	Milestone Due Date	Milestone Status	Last Quarter	Owner	Anticipated Barriers or Other Issues Related to Milestone Completion
Identify exemplar scientific and engineering assets that feature evaluation to serve as models for STEM Engagement activities	12/2013	Complete	N/A	IWG-Engagement	No barriers identified
Identify audiences that should receive STEM Engagement resources and programs	02/2014	Complete	N/A	IWG-Engagement	No barriers identified
Identify evaluation models used to effectively study engagement	09/2014	In Process	N/A	IWG-Engagement	No barriers identified
Identify STEM Engagement Activities of CO-STEM agencies	07/2014	In Process	N/A	IWG-Engagement	No barriers identified
Implementation of agency commitments related to Making and student engagement announced by President Obama at the White House Maker Faire.	06/2015	In Process	N/A	IWG-Engagement	No barriers identified

24

Q2 Update - Work Plan Sub-goal 3: Undergraduate STEM Education

- Implementation of evidence-based instructional practices and innovations
- Improve STEM education at 2-year colleges and transfer to 4-year colleges
- Support the development of university-industry partnerships to provide relevant and authentic experiences
- Address high failure rates in introductory mathematics at undergraduate

Key Milestones (Lead: NSF/TBD)	Milestone Due Date	Milestone Status	Last Quarter	Owner	Anticipated Barriers or Other Issues Related to Milestone Completion
Develop shared resource on research-base on undergraduate authentic science experiences	09/2014	On track	N/A	IWG Undergrad	No barriers identified
Share evaluation instruments for undergraduate authentic STEM experiences, including mentoring evaluation instruments	08/2014	On track	N/A	IWG Undergrad	No barriers identified
Identify common evaluation elements for undergraduate authentic STEM experiences to be used across federal agencies	10/2015	On track	N/A	IWG Undergrad	Potential obstacles include range of purposes motivating agency commitment to undergraduate research and intern opportunities.

25

Q2 Update - Work Plan Sub-goal 4: Under-represented Groups in STEM Fields

- Be more responsive to rapidly changing demographics
- Focus investments
- Invest in efforts to create campus climates that are effective in improving success for students from underrepresented groups

Key Milestones (Lead: NIH/NSF)	Milestone Due Date	Milestone Status	Last Quarter	Owner	Anticipated Barriers or Other Issues Related to Milestone Completion
Ideas proposed to maximize the impact of the federal investment with a timeline for agency adoption	10/2014	On track	N/A	IWG URG	No barriers identified
Agencies identify and begin implementation of modifications to existing program portfolio to address gaps to provide more opportunities for URMs in STEM	01/2015	On track	N/A	IWG URG	No barriers identified
Agencies identify strategies and timeline for incorporating campus climate guidelines and best practices into funding opportunities	06/2015	On track	N/A	IWG URG	No barriers identified

26

Q2 Update - Work Plan Sub-goal 5: Graduate STEM Education

- Recognize and provide financial support to students of high potential
- Provide opportunities for fellows' preparation in areas critical to the Nation
- Combine and enhance mechanisms that evaluate the impact of fellowships to inform future federal investments

Key Milestones (Lead: NSF/NIH)	Milestone Due Date	Milestone Status	Last Quarter	Owner	Anticipated Barriers or Other Issues Related to Milestone Completion
Assemble inventory of evaluation approaches for graduate programs	01/2015	On track	N/A	IWG Grad	No barriers identified
Identify available resources for the evaluation of graduate programs	01/2015	On track	N/A	IWG Grad	No barriers identified
Identify options such as courses and internships to enhance the quality of graduate training to better address the needs of a future STEM workforce	01/2015	On track	N/A	IWG Grad	No barriers identified

27

Key Indicators

Key Implementation Data

Indicator	Source	Baseline	Target?	Frequency	Latest data	Trend
Percentage of high school mathematics and science teachers who hold degrees in their teaching field or in science of mathematics education	Science and Engineering Indicators (S&EI) 2014	2012 (See slide 31)	N/A	Reported in S&EI 2014 biannually but based on variable survey	2012	
Number of STEM bachelor's degrees earned annually	S&EI 2014	554,365 (See slides 32 and 33)	N/A	Biannually	2011	Increasing
Percentage of bachelor's degrees awarded to women, black or African American, Hispanic, and American Indian or Alaska Native students	S&EI 2014	2011 (See slides 34-37)	N/A	Biannually	2011	Increasing

Indicators in Development:

Potential High Level Indicator	Potential Target Areas
• Teachers' science and mathematics content knowledge for teaching • Number of STEM graduate students at institutions by mechanism of support and supporting federal agency	

28

Teachers' Science and Mathematics Content Knowledge for Teaching

The Education and Human Resources (EHR) Directorate partnered with NSF's National Center for Science and Engineering Statistics (NCSES) in the Directorate of the Social, Behavioral, and Economic Sciences (SBE) to develop a two-year task, awarded to SRI, to provide insight on ways to reconfigure the K-12 chapter in the biennial *Science and Engineering Indicators* (SEI) that incorporates, over time, the 14 indicators identified in the *Monitoring Progress* report. Indicator 6 is **Teachers' science and mathematics content knowledge for teaching.** SRI created a "roadmap" of indicators available in the short-term, as well as those that will require further research and development:

Currently Available Data
• Data from Hill (Harvard) and the MET Project
• Teacher perceptions of preparedness from NAEP, TIMSS, and NSSME
• B&B, HSLS, and TALIS data on college coursework

Near-Term Activities
• Assemble and compare existing survey data and data from Hill and MET studies
• Review and synthesize what is known about correlations between these measures and student achievement

Long-Term Activities
• Develop instruments to measure teacher content knowledge for teaching for science and high school math
• Develop non-survey measures to get at knowledge in use

Additional Research Needs
• Relationship between college backgrounds and self-reports of preparedness and direct assessments of content knowledge for teaching
• Cost-effective measures for direct assessments at scale

Contributing Programs

The Federal Science, Technology, Engineering, and Mathematics (STEM) Portfolio is a report from the Federal Inventory of STEM Education Fast-Track Action Committee that was published in December 2011.

The inventory details Federal agencies' spending on STEM education and differs from previous such inventories in several ways.

• A consistent unit of analysis was used across all agencies (henceforth labeled as an "investment");
• the design and implementation of the inventory survey included extensive agency involvement; and
• a more thorough and detailed characterization of each agency's investments was obtained.

The result of these differences is a clearer and more complete picture of the Federal investment in STEM education than has previously been available.

http://www.whitehouse.gov/sites/default/files/microsites/ostp/costem__federal_stem_education_portfolio_report_1.pdf

Mathematics and Science Teachers with an Undergraduate or Graduate Degree in Mathematics or Science, by Grade Level (2012)

Mathematics and science teachers with an undergraduate or graduate degree in mathematics or science, by grade level: 2012

(Percent)

Grade level	Mathematics teachers' degree				Science teachers' degree			
	Mathematics	Mathematics education	Mathematics or mathematics education	None of these fields	Science or engineering	Science education	Science, engineering, or science education	None of these fields
Elementary	4	2	4	96	4	2	5	95
Middle	23	26	35	65	26	27	41	59
High	52	54	73	27	61	48	82	18

SOURCE: Banilower ER, Smith PS, Weiss IR, Malzahn KA, Campbell KM, Weis AM, *Report of the 2012 National Survey of Science and Mathematics Education* (2013).

31

Number of STEM Bachelor's Degrees Earned Annually (2011)

S&E degrees awarded, by degree level, Carnegie institution type, and field: 2011

Degree and institution type	All fields	All S&E	Agricultural sciences	Biological sciences	Computer sciences	Earth, atmospheric, and ocean sciences	Mathematics	Physical sciences	Psychology	Social sciences	Engineering
						S&E field					
Bachelor's	1,734,229	554,365	22,759	93,654	43,586	5,299	18,021	19,198	101,568	172,181	78,099
Doctorate-granting universities—very high research activity	444,695	210,425	10,283	37,626	8,193	2,023	6,682	6,852	28,402	69,114	41,250
Doctorate-granting universities—high research activity	249,963	82,410	3,812	13,668	4,909	869	2,176	2,490	13,832	23,135	17,519
Doctoral/research universities	121,588	30,818	874	4,391	4,231	265	835	964	5,389	10,657	3,212
Master's colleges and universities	647,346	158,483	5,162	24,340	16,319	1,397	5,677	5,614	40,877	47,776	11,321
Baccalaureate colleges	199,039	64,878	2,577	12,804	5,554	728	2,626	3,206	12,620	21,163	3,600
Associate's colleges	6,079	845	33	21	778	0	0	0	6	1	6
Medical schools and medical centers	6,435	66	0	66	0	0	0	0	0	0	0
Schools of engineering	1,329	1,168	0	5	41	14	9	25	0	2	1,072
Other specialized institutions	48,610	3,929	0	623	2,679	0	5	37	320	204	61
Tribal colleges	230	68	18	0	2	0	0	0	3	45	0
Not classified	8,915	1,275	0	110	880	3	11	10	119	84	58

NOTES: Medical and other health sciences are included in non-S&E. Carnegie institution type corresponds to the 2010 Carnegie Classification of Academic Institutions.

SOURCES: National Center for Education Statistics, Integrated Postsecondary Education Data System, Completions Survey; National Science Foundation, National Center for Science and Engineering Statistics, Integrated Science and Engineering Resources Data System (WebCASPAR), http://webcaspar.nsf.gov.

Science and Engineering Indicators 2014

32

Bachelor's Degrees by Broad Field of Degree: 2000-11

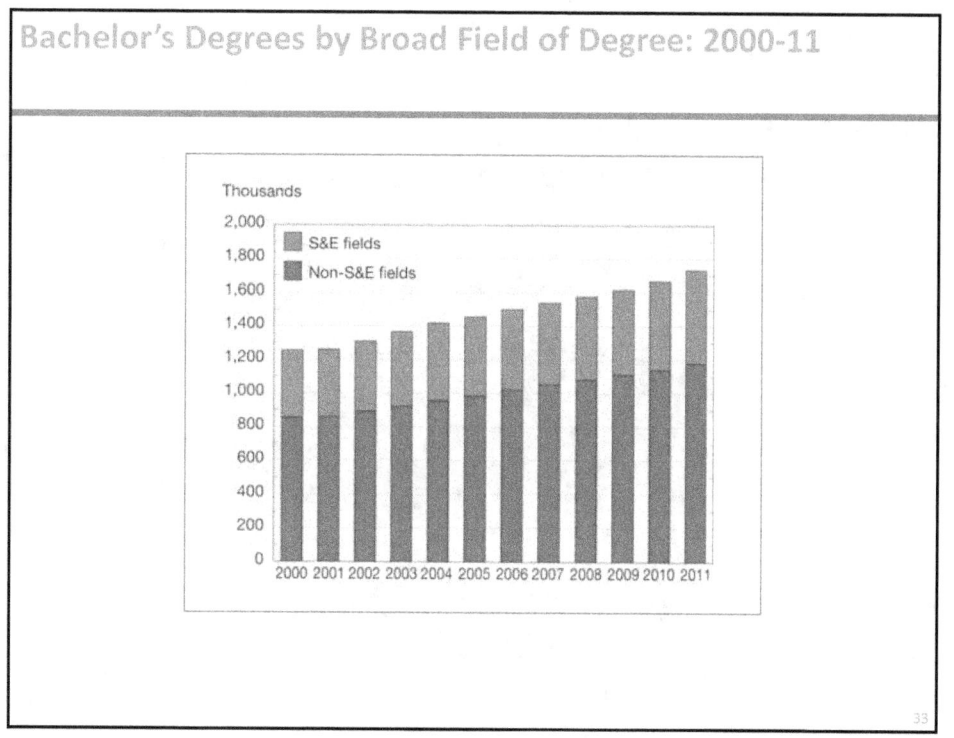

Percentage of Bachelor's Degrees Awarded to Women

Women's share of S&E bachelor's degrees, by field: 2000–11

(Percent)

Year	Physical sciences	Biological/agricultural sciences	Mathematics	Computer sciences	Psychology	Social sciences	Engineering
2000	40.8	55.8	47.8	28.0	76.5	54.2	20.5
2001	41.6	57.3	48.0	27.6	77.5	54.8	20.1
2002	42.7	58.6	46.9	27.5	77.5	54.8	20.9
2003	41.7	59.7	45.6	27.0	77.7	54.7	20.3
2004	42.2	60.1	45.9	25.1	77.8	54.5	20.5
2005	42.6	59.9	44.6	22.3	77.8	54.2	20.0
2006	42.2	59.8	44.9	20.7	77.4	53.7	19.5
2007	41.1	58.6	43.9	18.6	77.4	53.8	18.5
2008	41.1	58.2	43.9	17.7	77.1	53.5	18.5
2009	41.0	58.2	43.0	17.9	77.2	53.6	18.1
2010	40.9	57.8	43.1	18.2	77.1	53.7	18.4
2011	40.3	58.1	43.0	17.7	77.0	54.2	18.8

NOTE: Physical sciences include earth, atmospheric, and ocean sciences.

SOURCES: National Center for Education Statistics, Integrated Postsecondary Education Data System, Completions Survey; National Science Foundation, National Center for Science and Engineering Statistics, WebCASPAR database, http://webcaspar.nsf.gov.

Science and Engineering Indicators 2014

Women's Share of S&E Bachelor's Degrees by Field: 2000-11

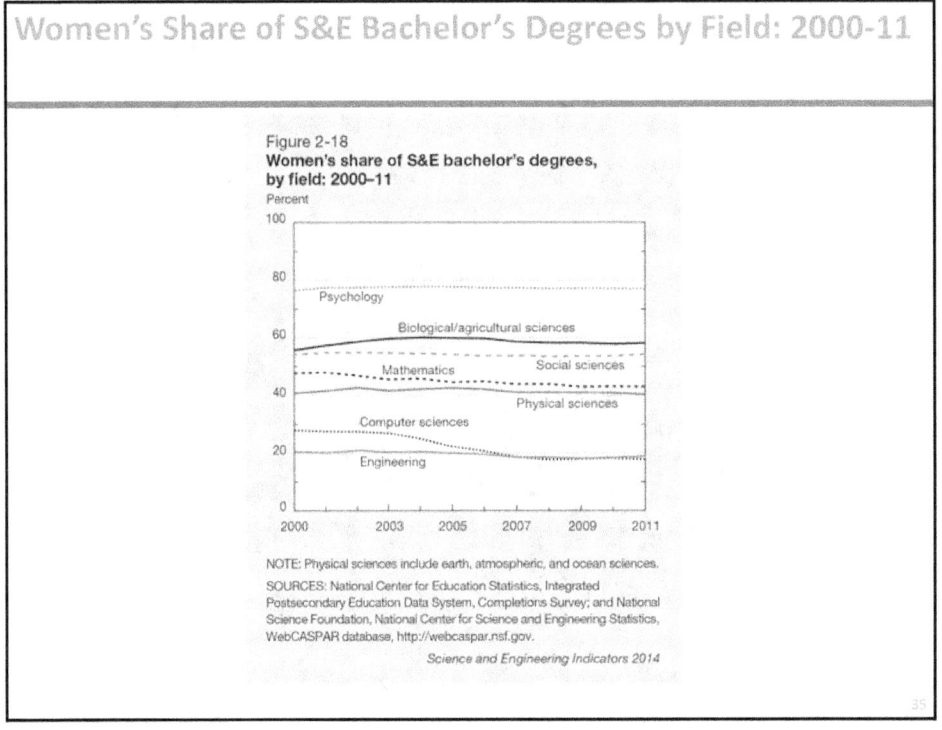

Figure 2-18
Women's share of S&E bachelor's degrees, by field: 2000–11

NOTE: Physical sciences include earth, atmospheric, and ocean sciences.

SOURCES: National Center for Education Statistics, Integrated Postsecondary Education Data System, Completions Survey; and National Science Foundation, National Center for Science and Engineering Statistics, WebCASPAR database, http://webcaspar.nsf.gov.

Science and Engineering Indicators 2014

Percentage of Bachelor's Degrees Awarded by Race and Ethnicity (2011)

Share of S&E bachelor's degrees among U.S. citizens and permanent residents, by race and ethnicity: 2000–11

(Percent)

Year	Asian or Pacific Islander	Black or African American	Hispanic	American Indian or Alaska Native	White
2000	9.3	8.6	7.3	0.7	70.5
2001	9.5	8.7	7.4	0.7	69.6
2002	9.4	8.7	7.5	0.7	69.2
2003	9.4	8.7	7.7	0.7	68.5
2004	9.4	8.8	7.7	0.7	67.7
2005	9.6	8.8	7.9	0.7	67.2
2006	9.7	8.7	8.0	0.7	67.1
2007	9.7	8.6	8.2	0.7	66.8
2008	9.9	8.6	8.5	0.7	66.1
2009	9.9	8.6	8.8	0.7	65.5
2010	9.9	8.6	9.1	0.7	64.4
2011	9.8	8.7	9.6	0.6	63.4

NOTES: Hispanic may be any race. American Indian or Alaska Native, Asian or Pacific Islander, black, or African American and white refer to individuals who are not of Hispanic origin. Percentages do not sum to 100 because data do not include individuals who did not report their race and ethnicity.

SOURCES: National Center for Education Statistics, Integrated Postsecondary Education Data System, Completions Survey; National Science Foundation, National Center for Science and Engineering Statistics, WebCASPAR database, http://webcaspar.nsf.gov.

Science and Engineering Indicators 2014

Share of S&E Bachelor's Degrees among U.S. Citizens and Permanent Residents by Race and Ethnicity: 2000-11

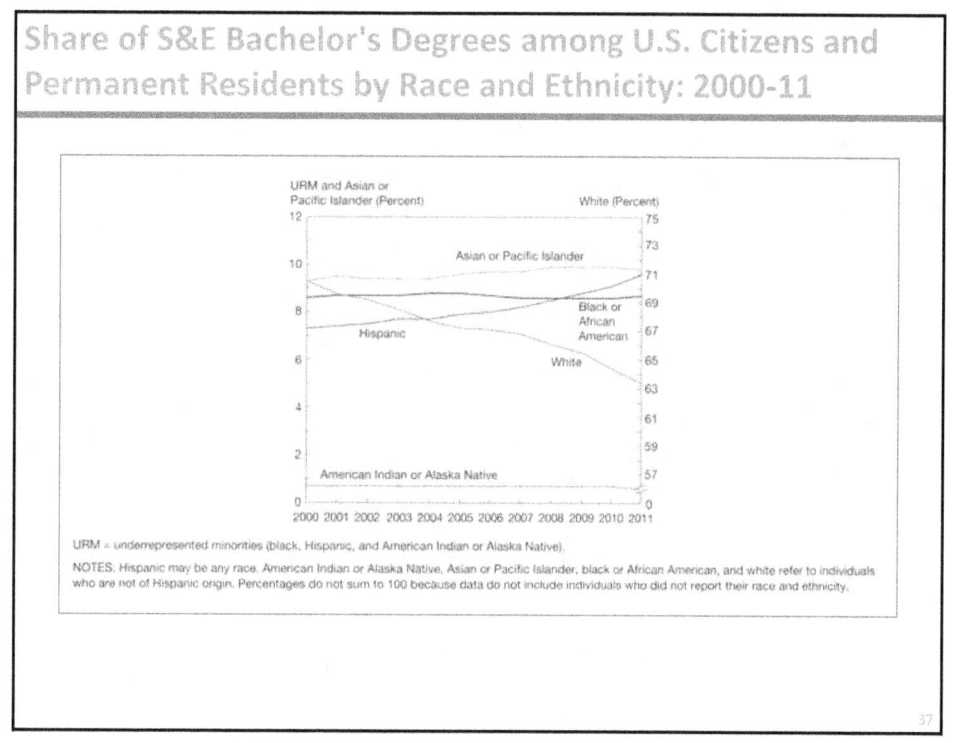

URM = underrepresented minorities (black, Hispanic, and American Indian or Alaska Native).

NOTES: Hispanic may be any race. American Indian or Alaska Native, Asian or Pacific Islander, black or African American, and white refer to individuals who are not of Hispanic origin. Percentages do not sum to 100 because data do not include individuals who did not report their race and ethnicity.